CW01208847

Peter Martyr Vermigli

by Simonetta Carr

with Illustrations by Joel Spector

REFORMATION HERITAGE BOOKS
Grand Rapids, Michigan

Peter Martyr Vermigli
© 2017 by Simonetta Carr

Cover artwork by Joel Spector

For additional artwork by Joel Spector, see pages 7, 9, 15, 19, 27, 29, 35, 37, 41, 49, 51.

All rights reserved. No part of this book may be used or reproduced in any manner whatsoever without written permission except in the case of brief quotations embodied in critical articles and reviews. Direct your requests to the publisher at the following address:

Reformation Heritage Books
2965 Leonard St. NE
Grand Rapids, MI 49525
616-977-0889 / Fax: 616-285-3246
e-mail: orders@heritagebooks.org
website: www.heritagebooks.org

Printed in the United States of America
17 18 19 20 21 22/10 9 8 7 6 5 4 3 2 1

Library of Congress Cataloging-in-Publication Data

Names: Carr, Simonetta, author. | Spector, Joel, 1949-2016, illustrator.
Title: Peter Martyr Vermigli / by Simonetta Carr ; with illustrations by Joel Spector.
Description: Grand Rapids, Michigan : Reformation Heritage Books, 2017. | Series: Christian biographies for young readers
Identifiers: LCCN 2016055296 | ISBN 9781601785145 (hardcover : alk. paper)
Subjects: LCSH: Vermigli, Pietro Martire, 1499-1562—Juvenile literature. | Reformation—Biography—Juvenile literature.
Classification: LCC BR350.V37 C37 2017 | DDC 270.6092 [B]—dc23 LC record available at https://lccn.loc.gov/2016055296

For additional Reformed literature, request a free book list from Reformation Heritage Books at the above address.

CHRISTIAN BIOGRAPHIES FOR YOUNG READERS

This series introduces children to important people in the Christian tradition. Parents and schoolteachers alike will welcome the excellent educational value it provides for students, while the quality of the publication and the artwork make each volume a keepsake for generations to come. Furthermore, the books in the series go beyond the simple story of someone's life by teaching young readers the historical and theological relevance of each character.

AVAILABLE VOLUMES OF THE SERIES
John Calvin
Augustine of Hippo
John Owen
Athanasius
Lady Jane Grey
Anselm of Canterbury
John Knox
Jonathan Edwards
Marie Durand
Martin Luther
Peter Martyr Vermigli

Table of Contents

Introduction 5

Chapter 1: A Desire to Teach the Scriptures 6

Chapter 2: Troubling Questions 14

Chapter 3: The Escape North 22

Chapter 4: The King's Summons 31

Chapter 5: A New Escape 39

Chapter 6: The Last Years 46

Time Line 54

Did You Know? 55

What Happened to the Others? 59

From Peter Martyr's Pen 63

Acknowledgments 64

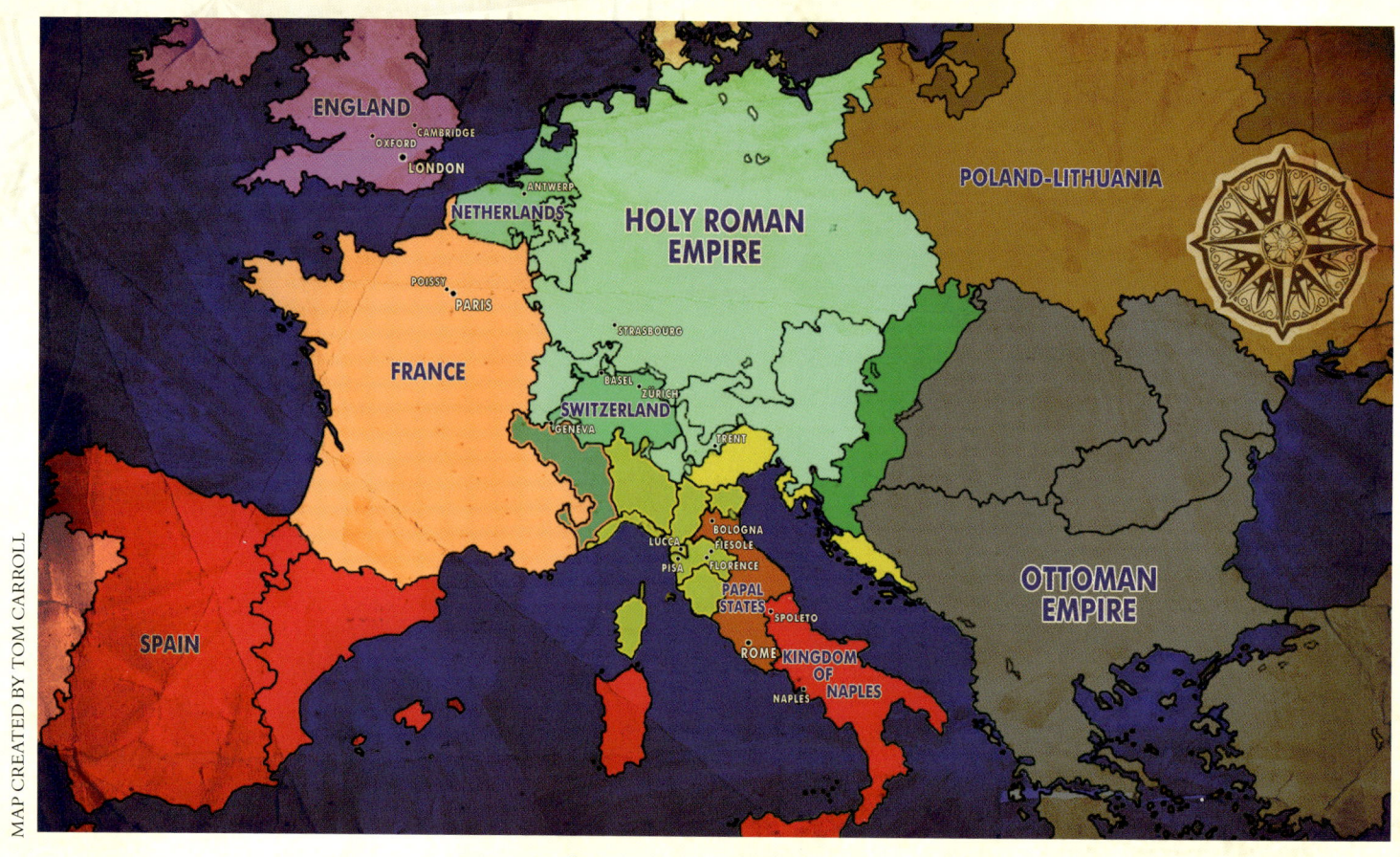

A map of Europe during Vermigli's life

Introduction

When he grew up, Peter Martyr Vermigli (pronounced Vayr-MEEL-yee) wanted to be a teacher of God's Word. Finally, after many years of diligent study, he became one of the most respected leaders of the Roman Catholic Church, the only type of church in Europe at that time. He taught and preached so well that people came from other cities to hear him.

In spite of his popularity, he felt more and more uncomfortable in his position, because he was forced to do, say, and teach things that he found contrary to the Bible. At the same time, the Roman Catholic Church became increasingly hostile against those who raised questions. His only option was to leave his position, his country, and his friends.

Peter Martyr Vermigli

CHAPTER ONE
A Desire to Teach the Scriptures

Peter Vermigli was born on September 8, 1499, in the city of Florence, Italy, one of the most important European centers for art, literature, and business at that time. His father, Stefano, had a profitable job making and selling shoes. Stefano and his wife, Maria, had been praying for a child for a long time. When Peter was born, Stefano was forty-three years old. Peter's birth filled his parents with joy. They gave him the middle name Mariano, probably in honor of Mary, the mother of Jesus. After Peter, the Vermiglis had two more children—Felicita and Antonio.

Peter's mother taught him to read and write both Italian and Latin, the language of ancient

Woodcut of sixteenth-century Florence. During Peter Vermigli's life, Florence was one of the richest and most prestigious cities in Europe and an important artistic center.

FROM THE NUREMBERG CHRONICLE, MICHEL WOLGEMUT, WILHELM PLEYDENWURFF (TEXT HARTMANN SCHEDEL), LICENSED UNDER PUBLIC DOMAIN VIA WIKIMEDIA COMMONS.

Peter's mother taught him to read and write both Italian and Latin.

A DESIRE TO TEACH THE SCRIPTURES

7

Rome that was still used in schools and churches all over Europe. When Peter grew a little older, his father sent him to a tutor who taught daily lessons to young people. Sadly, Maria died when Peter was twelve. It must have been very painful for him.

Peter was a bright student. He also enjoyed attending worship at the local church, where he assisted the priest and helped to keep the church clean. In the meantime, he tried to learn as much as possible about the Bible. His dream was to study the Scriptures and teach them to others.

Stefano was not happy with Peter's wishes. He probably wanted his son to earn a lot of money, marry, and raise a family to continue the Vermigli name, but Peter never changed his mind. After Peter turned fifteen, his father finally gave him permission to enter a monastery in the small town of Fiesole, five miles northeast of Florence. A monastery is a place where churchmen called monks, or friars, live together to devote their life to good works and prayer.

The monastery of Fiesole (Badia Fiesolana), where Peter Martyr started his religious life. Some of the buildings were added later.

Peter assisted the priest and helped to keep the local church clean.

A DESIRE TO TEACH THE SCRIPTURES

9

PETER MARTYR VERMIGLI

Usually when people joined a monastery, they changed their names to mark their new life. Peter changed his middle name from Mariano to Martyr, after another Peter who had died a martyr. He used this name until he died, and many of his friends simply called him Martyr, so we will use this name for the rest of the story.

Martyr continued to study hard and took full advantage of the monastery's library—the best in the territory of Florence. After two years, his superiors, impressed by his intelligence, sent him to the University of Padua in the north of Italy, one of the most ancient and prestigious schools in Europe. There, he studied for eight years, perfecting old subjects and learning new ones, including Greek and the works of early Christian writers.

PIETRO BELLINI, FLICKR

La Specula Tower over the Bacchiglione River in Padua. In Vermigli's time, it was part of a castle. It later became an astronomical observatory. Today, it is a museum.

Around that time, a German friar named Martin Luther was making news all over Europe with some writings that challenged the authority of the pope (the head of the Roman Catholic Church). Martyr probably talked about these issues with other students, who were some of the most brilliant minds at that time.

After his graduation, Martyr was ordained a priest and began to preach in different Italian cities. His dream of teaching God's Word to others had come true. He was a good preacher, and people loved to listen to his sermons. At the same time, he was sad to see that many people knew hardly anything about the Bible, while many church leaders who had great training and experience preached only when they could get honors and riches.

Martin Luther
REFORMATION ART, WWW.REFORMATIONART.COM/

A DESIRE TO TEACH THE SCRIPTURES

"Christ's sheep are either starving, or poorly and badly fed," he wrote later. "Usually there is preaching only during the brief period of Lent [forty days before Easter].... During the rest of the year, the churches devote themselves only to processions, shouts, songs, and music, without a word to edify the poor people."

To teach the Bible correctly, Martyr knew it was important to study it in the languages in which it was originally written—Hebrew and Greek. He had already studied Greek in Padua. In 1530, when he moved to the city of Bologna, he hired a Jewish physician named Isaac to teach him Hebrew, and he studied hard for three years.

In 1533 he was sent to run a monastery in Spoleto—about 130 miles south of his native Florence. In his new position, he was able to do more to make improvements in the church and worked with other church leaders who shared his concerns. About four years later, however, he was moved again—this time to a monastery in Naples (about one hundred miles south of Rome), where his life changed forever.

A view of the area around Spoleto

A DESIRE TO TEACH THE SCRIPTURES

CHAPTER TWO

Troubling Questions

Once again, Martyr met people who cared deeply about the problems in the church. This time, however, along with church leaders there were professors, noblemen, and noblewomen. They had different views but were united by a sincere desire to bring the church back to the pure teachings of the Scriptures. They met to discuss their ideas in gardens, in someone's home, or on the beach.

With these friends, Martyr learned about the changes that were happening north of the Alps. By this time, Martin Luther was openly teaching that people, by God's grace, should simply believe by faith in the gospel—the good news of Christ's life, death, and resurrection—without trying to merit God's favor.

Castel dell'Ovo, one of the oldest fortifications in the Gulf of Naples, was probably a familiar scene for Martyr.

In Naples, Martyr met a group of people who cared deeply about problems in the church.

TROUBLING QUESTIONS

15

Many people were following Luther's teachings. Especially in Germany and Switzerland, books were being published to explain the good news of salvation through faith alone in Jesus Christ alone. In Naples, Martyr was able to read some of these books, even though the Roman Catholic Church had banned them. The church authorities were afraid that as people read them, they would become so confident of God's favor that they would stop obeying His laws. Luther instead encouraged people to obey God out of gratefulness for His grace, and not out of fear or to try to gain some merit.

Martyr compared these books with the Scriptures and found them to be in agreement. He learned more every day. At first he felt like the blind man in Mark 8:24. Even though Jesus had given the man sight, he still saw things a little unclearly. This feeling didn't stop Martyr from sharing what he had learned. "When my Heavenly Father, through the merits of Christ, had compassion on me," he said, "I began to see through a cloud, and as trees walking, the truth of the Gospel; nor, though I understood as yet but darkly, could I keep silent. I communicated it unto others, and the light was increased."

Martyr had to be careful when he preached. The pope had already condemned Luther and excluded him from the Roman Catholic Church. Finally, one of Martyr's sermons got him in trouble when he contradicted one of the church's teachings. The church had used a portion of Paul's letter to the Corinthians to prove the existence of purgatory—a place between heaven and hell where, in their view, people with lesser sins went after death to get purified before going to heaven. Martyr read that portion carefully in the original Greek language, compared it with the teachings of the church fathers, and still did not believe that text talked about such a place. In good conscience, he preached what he believed to be right.

Immediately, someone reported him to the higher authorities, and he was suspended from preaching. It was a difficult punishment for him, because preaching the gospel had always been his greatest desire. Thankfully, he had many friends in Rome who worked close to the pope and were able have this decision revoked.

Soon, Martyr's superiors decided to move him again. They needed someone to lead a monastery in the independent city-state of Lucca (near Florence), and Martyr seemed to be the right person. To his joy, Martyr discovered that the teachings of Luther and other Reformers had already spread in Lucca, and many people wanted to learn more about the Bible.

Encouraged by this interest, he opened a Bible school for older children, young people, and adults in his monastery. He hired good teachers of Greek, Hebrew, Latin, and theology (the study of God) and explained Paul's letters and the Psalms daily. There had never been a school like this in all of Italy. The school was well received, so much so that the local authorities asked Martyr's superiors to keep him in Lucca even after the end of his term.

In spite of this, Martyr was uncomfortable with many ceremonies he had to perform such as the Mass—the Roman Catholic lifting of the bread and wine, when the priest offers Jesus to the Father as an "unbloody sacrifice."

Church of San Frediano, Lucca

Martyr was uncomfortable with many ceremonies he had to perform.

TROUBLING QUESTIONS

From the Scriptures, Martyr understood that Jesus has sacrificed Himself once and for all on the cross, and we only have to receive this by faith. That's what he wanted to teach, or at least discuss, but he was not allowed to do it. Even worse, as a supervisor he had to ask other priests to perform the same ceremony, as well as other rituals he found contrary to the Scriptures.

Like many other people in Italy, he kept hoping the church would change. His friends in Rome were still trying to influence other church leaders, and some meetings were held to find a middle way between the teachings of Luther and those held by most church leaders in Rome, including the pope. Soon, it became obvious that in some things there couldn't be a middle way. Either Christ has done everything to merit our salvation, or we still need to merit it somehow.

Things got worse when a church leader, Gian Pietro Carafa, reopened a legal court to arrest and try anyone who seemed to be following Luther's teachings. He was particularly concerned about Lucca, which was considered the most contaminated place of all. Fearing punishment from the pope, the government of Lucca, which had been favorable to Martyr, sided with Carafa.

The leaders of Martyr's monastic order invited him to Genoa, on the west coast of Italy, to discuss the situation. In reality, they wanted to question him about his teachings. Warned by some friends, he had to face a difficult decision. He could continue to perform the Roman Catholic ceremonies, pretending to agree, but that would have gone against his conscience. To live according to his understanding of the Scriptures, there was only one thing he could do—leave Italy.

Gian Pietro Carafa

CHAPTER THREE
The Escape North

Martyr shared his plans with his most reliable companions and made sure everything in the monastery was in order, then left on horseback with three of his closest friends, taking with him his most important papers. He asked another friend to send him the rest of his books. His first stop was the nearby city of Pisa. There he was able to celebrate the Lord's Supper as he believed Christ had instituted it—both as a remembrance of Christ's sacrifice and a spiritual communion with Him in heaven.

Strengthened by this sacrament, Martyr and his three friends traveled north, passing by his native city of Florence and visiting briefly the monastery in Fiesole. There, he wrote a letter to his church in Lucca, explaining his decision. Along the way, he also wrote letters to his friends in Rome and a letter to his superiors, sending back the ring he wore as a sign of his office. Finally, he crossed the Alps, never to return.

THE ESCAPE NORTH

Martyr crossed the Alps, never to return.

It was summer, so the journey was not as difficult and dangerous as it would have been in the winter. It took about a month for the four men to arrive at their destination—Zurich, Switzerland—where a strong Protestant church was thriving. The leaders of that church welcomed the Italians warmly. They were already aware of Martyr's reputation for biblical knowledge and sound teaching. At the moment, however, they couldn't offer him a teaching position. After two days, the four friends moved together into a small lodging in the nearby city of Basel.

A view of today's Basel, with the medieval bridge Martyr probably crossed several times
MARIANO MANTEL, FLICKR

Martyr had mixed feelings. He was deeply grateful to God, who had kept him safe from danger and had led him to a place where others openly shared his convictions about God and the Scriptures. On the other hand, he missed his country and his friends. "I am not made of brass, nor is my flesh of iron," he wrote later to another Reformer.

He also wondered if going to Zurich had been the right decision. Maybe he should have gone to Geneva, where other Italians had moved. Without any prospects of work as a teacher, he felt anxious and worried.

Within weeks, however, God's plan became clear. The college at Strasbourg, about eighty miles north of Basel, needed a professor of Old Testament studies. Someone suggested Martyr, who accepted gladly. During his first seventeen days in Strasbourg, he stayed as a guest of a well-known pastor and teacher named Martin Bucer. Martyr had already read and appreciated Bucer's writings and felt honored to live in his house.

Martin Bucer
REFORMATION ART, WWW.REFORMATIONART.COM

The admiration was mutual. "A man has arrived from Italy who is quite learned in Greek, Hebrew, and Latin and well skilled in the Scriptures," Bucer wrote to his friend John Calvin. "He is forty-four years old, serious in character and of keen judgment. His name is Peter Martyr."

Martyr learned much by watching Bucer and his family. Their house was always busy and full of people. Many, like Martyr, were refugees from other Roman Catholic countries. Since priests and monks were not allowed to marry, it was the first time that Martyr could watch the family life of a minister of the gospel. Bucer was busy preaching and caring for the people in his church, but he also worked hard with his wife, Wibrandis, to keep the home running. To him, raising a family was an important calling from God.

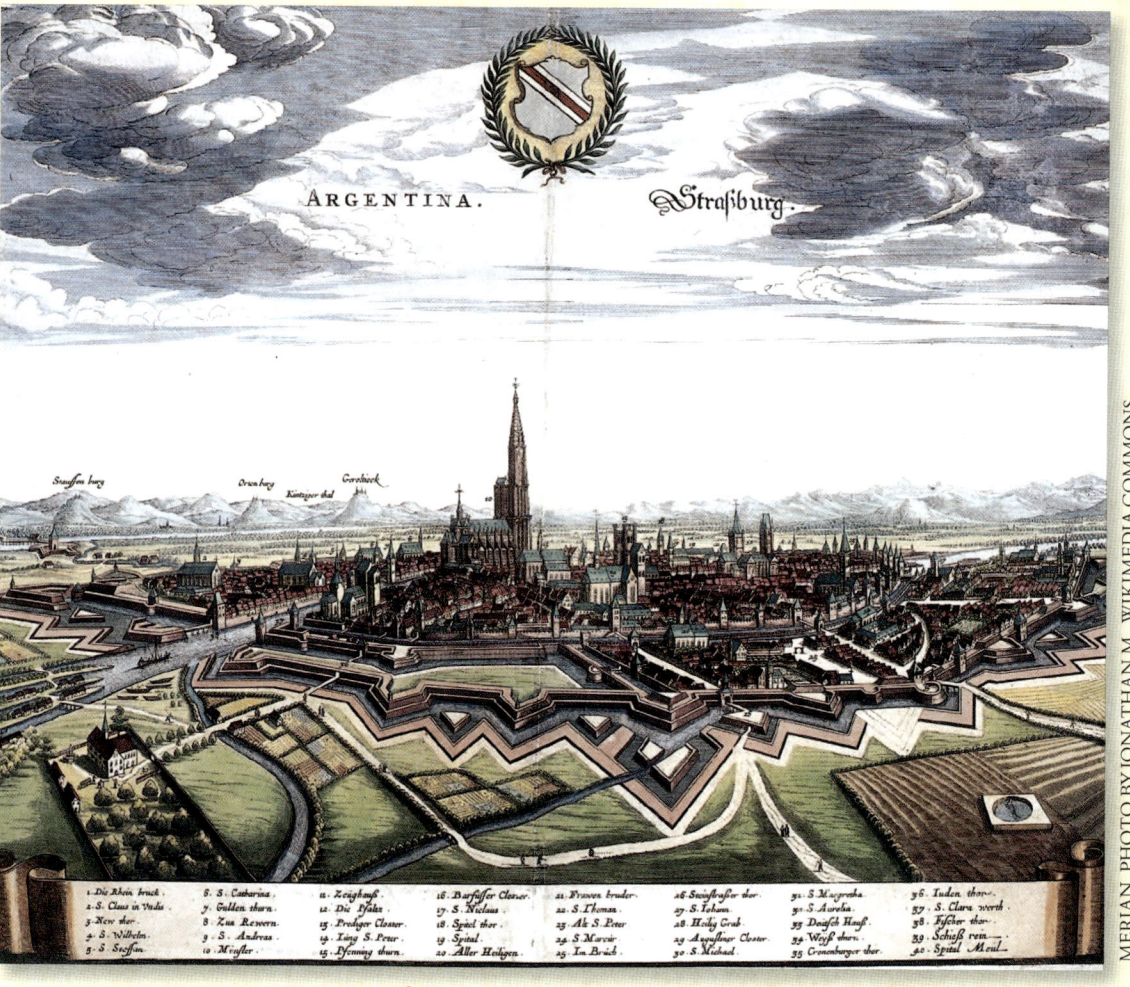

A map of Strasbourg, as seen in 1644

In Strasbourg, for the first time Martyr watched the family life of a minister of the gospel.

THE ESCAPE NORTH

27

PETER MARTYR VERMIGLI

So far, everything Martyr had seen in the churches in Zurich and Strasbourg had filled him with joy. Before leaving Italy, he had sometimes wondered if he were chasing a dream—if the reformation of the church was just an ideal "which can be clearly understood but doesn't really exist anywhere." The Christians in Switzerland and Germany had proved his doubts wrong.

Soon, Martyr gained a reputation as an excellent teacher. His lectures were clear and well organized, and he always stayed on topic. Also, his naturally calm personality helped him to keep order when the students started to argue. He especially impressed his listeners with his great knowledge of the Bible, ancient languages, early Christian writings, and classical literature. Many students came from other cities. He must have been especially happy when someone arrived from Italy or brought him news from his country. In fact, eighteen people from his church in Lucca left Italy within the first year after his departure and moved to places where they could worship God freely.

Strasbourg today
RAPHAEL REINS, FLICKR

Martyr was an excellent teacher.

THE ESCAPE NORTH

29

Charles V

Once he was settled in his teaching job, Martyr decided to start a family, so some friends introduced him to a respectable French lady named Catherine Dammartin. Catherine came from a noble family but had spent many years in a convent as a nun. Martyr and Catherine enjoyed a happy marriage. Martyr discovered that she was God-fearing, loving, generous, and hardworking. The couple probably communicated in Latin, because Martyr didn't speak French and Catherine didn't speak Italian.

Soon, however, the couple's happiness was marred by wars and fears. For about fifteen years, the Protestant princes of Germany had been united in an alliance (called the Schmalkaldic League) to protect their territories from the Roman Catholic emperor Charles V, whose ultimate goal was to unite the empire under the religion of Rome. In 1546, some disunity among the princes allowed the emperor to attack them, until he crushed their armies in battle.

CHAPTER FOUR

The King's Summons

Strengthened by his victory, the emperor started a new policy, demanding that Protestants adopt many ceremonies of the Roman Catholic Church. The policy (called the Augsburg Interim) was supposed to be temporary while the leaders of that church met in the city of Trent (now in northern Italy) to make permanent decisions.

Some Protestants thought they should conform to the emperor's will, while many others, including Bucer, were against it. Martyr didn't have to make that choice, because in 1547 Thomas Cranmer, archbishop of Canterbury, the highest authority of the Church of England after the king, invited him to his country. Encouraged by his local church, Martyr moved to England with his friend and assistant Julius Terentianus, who had left Italy with him and had faithfully stayed by his side. Catherine and others followed later.

Archbishop Thomas Cranmer

As in many other countries in those days, the people of England had to adopt the religion of their ruler. Their new king, ten-year-old Edward VI, was a committed Protestant, but England had been influenced by the Roman Catholic Church for so long that the people had a hard time changing. Cranmer was convinced that God's Spirit works in people's hearts through the preaching of the gospel, but he didn't have enough well-trained preachers to send around the country. That is why he called some of the best teachers in Europe. He assigned Martyr to the University of Oxford. Two years later, he invited Bucer to teach at the University of Cambridge.

Martyr discovered that even some of the teachers and students in Oxford were opposed to changes. In his lectures, he explained that Protestants were not teaching anything new. They were just going back to what the original apostles had preached.

Edward VI, silver medal
NATIONAL GALLERY OF ART, GIFT OF LISA UNGER BASKIN

One of the main disagreements was over the Lord's Supper. The Roman Catholic Church taught (and it still does today) that when a priest raised the bread and wine, those objects became the body and blood of Christ, even if they still looked like bread and wine. Martyr had some documents to prove that this was not the original teaching of the church. It had become official only after twelve hundred years of Christianity. He encouraged his students to stay faithful to the Bible. In his lectures, he explained that bread and wine stay bread and wine, but when we eat them in faith, the Holy Spirit lifts our souls to Christ and unites us with Him. He debated this subject well and won the trust of many students.

Tom Quad, the largest courtyard of Christ Church College, in Oxford, where Martyr lived for some time after 1551

FR LAWRENCE LEW, O.P.

Other people continued to oppose him. Things got worse when Catherine arrived. To many people, the marriage of an ex-monk to an ex-nun was offensive, especially since each of them had vowed to stay single. Protestants believed those vows were not biblical, so they didn't count. Some Roman Catholics were rude to Catherine, calling her names and making fun of her large size. Many of the common people, however, loved her because she was generous toward the poor and gave help and advice to women who were sick or having babies.

In the meantime, the people of England were suffering from a series of bad harvests, and the poor kept getting poorer. Also, the loss of religious ceremonies and monasteries they had trusted for years made people insecure. When the king demanded the use of a new manual for worship in English and not in Latin, called the Book of Common Prayer, many people's frustrations mounted into a violent rebellion. They were used to Latin, even if they didn't understand everything.

Wheat fields in the Oxfordshire. When Martyr was in England, over 95 percent of the English population lived on farms and depended on the fruits of their harvest.
ERIC HARDY, FLICKR

Catherine was generous toward the poor and gave help and advice to women who were sick or having babies.

THE KING'S SUMMONS

35

Martyr knew that changes are always scary and the people just needed to be taught and reassured, but at the moment there was no time to do it. He was in great danger. Some students smashed his windows with rocks, and others sent him death threats. To save his life, he had to move to London under royal escort, leaving Catherine and the family's helpers in the safe care of friends. He missed Catherine, but found comfort in knowing they were still united. In fact, he used the example of a man in London with his wife in Oxford to explain how a believer on earth is united to Christ, who is in heaven.

Finally, the situation became more peaceful, and he was able to return to Oxford, but his sorrows were not over. In 1551 his dear friend Bucer died, after many illnesses aggravated by the cold and damp English climate. "As long as Bucer was in England or while we lived together in Germany, I never felt myself to be in exile," Martyr wrote to Bucer's wife, Wibrandis.

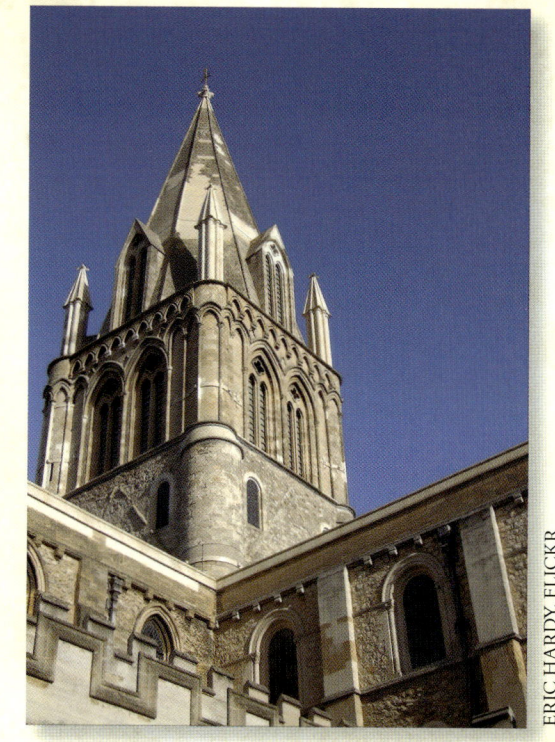

Christ Church's Tower, Oxford

Martyr's windows were often smashed with rocks, and he received death threats.

THE KING'S SUMMONS

37

The hardest blow came two years later. Just as things had begun to improve in Oxford and in most of the country, Catherine died from a recurring fever that had afflicted her for a long time. Martyr, who suffered from the same illness, called the pain of losing his wife "hardly bearable," even though he had the comfort of knowing she was happy in heaven.

A third shock during the same year was the sudden death of King Edward VI, perhaps from a respiratory infection. He was only seventeen years old. Before dying, he signed a legal document that left the throne to his cousin, sixteen-year-old Lady Jane Grey, but his half sister Mary, convinced she was the rightful heir, dethroned Jane less than two weeks later and proclaimed herself queen. Jane and her husband were imprisoned and eventually beheaded.

A medal by Jacopo Nizzola da Trezzo, portraying Queen Mary I of England
NATIONAL GALLERY OF ART, ALISA MELLON BRUCE FUND

CHAPTER FIVE

A New Escape

Initially, the new government ordered Martyr not to leave the country. Later, they forbade him to leave his house and placed a guard to watch him. Martyr expected to die, and some of his enemies wished for his death. In the meantime, Martyr's friend Julius went to London to appeal to the queen. Since Martyr had come to England at the request of the English government, Mary's counselors finally agreed to let him leave, and he moved to London to wait for the official papers.

In London, Cranmer was overjoyed to see his friend. He had just distributed a lot of posters all over the city inviting people to a public discussion of the Book of Common Prayer, and he asked Martyr to help him. He thought the book could be kept, even under Mary's government, allowing the people to pray and worship in their own language, instead of in Latin. Martyr, who had worked with Cranmer on the editing of this book, was glad to assist him.

The entrance to Lambeth Palace (Morton Gate). As archbishop of the Church of England, Cranmer lived at Lambeth until he was imprisoned.

Instead of allowing the discussion, however, the government ordered Cranmer to appear before the highest court of law. Cranmer knew what this meant. The next day, after dining with Martyr, he spoke to him in private, saying they would never meet again in this life. He advised Martyr to flee the country if his permit didn't arrive soon. As expected, the court sent Cranmer to the prison in the Tower of London, where other Protestants were kept.

Martyr's permit, signed by Mary, arrived five days later. Being able to escape prison and death still seemed like a dream. It only became reality when he boarded the boat. To avoid any danger in the areas of the empire loyal to the Roman Catholic Church, he spread the word he was sailing to Hamburg, Germany, when instead he sailed to Antwerp, Belgium. He advised Julius to leave later with a different boat. To their surprise, the boats arrived in Antwerp at the same time.

A 1572 map of the city of Antwerp, with boats coming and going, from Georg Braun and Frans Hogenberg's atlas

Cranmer told Martyr they would never meet again in this life.

From Antwerp, the two friends traveled together to Strasbourg on the River Rhine. The trip was full of dangers, including encounters with a deadly disease and with troops of soldiers. Thankfully, the weather was mild, and they arrived in Strasbourg safe and sound. There, Martyr went back to his teaching position eagerly.

He received a letter from Cranmer only fifteen months after his arrival. The letter was not signed because Cranmer had to have it smuggled out of prison, but Martyr recognized the handwriting. Cranmer explained he was under strict guard and had written to no one else. In spite of his suffering and the difficult condition of the church, he was sure of God's ultimate victory for His people. That was the last letter Cranmer wrote. On March 21, 1556, he was burned at the stake. Martyr treasured the letter for the rest of his life.

The Rhine River in autumn. Martyr traveled in November. In those days, river travel was usually faster and safer than road travel.

In the meantime, instead of uniting Protestants and Roman Catholics, as some people had hoped, the church council that had been meeting at Trent made the division between them even sharper. In 1555, when Charles V left the throne, his successor, Ferdinand I, allowed each prince to declare his own region either Roman Catholic or Lutheran. To worship according to conscience, a

A session of the Council of Trent

Lutheran living under a Roman Catholic prince would have to move to a region ruled by a Lutheran, and vice versa.

Problems continued. Moving was not as easy then as it usually is today. And not all Protestants were Lutheran. Some had different ideas, especially about the celebration of the Lord's Supper. Martyr and other Reformers believed that many issues were not worth arguing about. The important thing was to hold the same beliefs regarding God and salvation from sin. At the same time, to worship together, Christians had to agree on the meaning of their worship and be convinced that it was according to the Scriptures.

Around that time, Martyr received some alarming news from Italy. Carafa, the archenemy of Protestants, had been elected pope under the name of Paul IV and had tightened all measures against Protestants. Even worse, some believers in Lucca had denied their Protestant faith for fear of being punished. "How shall I keep from crying and lamenting," Martyr wrote to their church, "when I see such a beautiful garden as was the church of my brethren at Lucca destroyed, scattered, and cast down in a single moment by such a terrible windstorm?"

He explained that all Christians must expect to be persecuted for their faith. If they are not, they should use their time to prepare for coming battles or to leave the country. "Why do you stay there?" he asked. "Your home? Your villa? Relatives? Wealth? The consolations of this world? So you value all these things more highly than you do God himself."

A NEW ESCAPE

Just when Martyr felt concerned for the church in Italy, he received an invitation to move closer to his country. Henry Bullinger, the main leader of the church in Zurich, asked him to teach the Old Testament in their prestigious school—one he had always admired.

Moving to Zurich would bring Martyr full circle to the day he had first arrived in Zurich, hoping to teach in Bullinger's school. Besides, he was glad to leave the school of Strasbourg, where there was too much disunity over religious matters. Despite the protests of the city and school of Strasbourg, Martyr moved to Zurich in July 1556.

Heinrich Bullinger
REFORMATION ART, WWW.REFORMATIONART.COM

CHAPTER SIX

The Last Years

Initially, Martyr stayed at Bullinger's house. Martyr and Bullinger had stayed in touch since they first met in 1542 and had become good friends. Five years younger than Martyr, Bullinger had been married for forty years to an ex-nun named Anna. The couple had eleven children, but three had died as infants. Like Bucer's home in Strasbourg, their home was filled with guests, students, and refugees.

After a few days, Martyr moved to a house near his friend where he was joined by Julius, his wife, and their children. Martyr was very close to Julius's family, and one of Julius's sons was named after him—Martyrillus (meaning "little Martyr"). Apparently, Martyrillus was well behaved, while another boy, Isaac, was quite a handful. "I can almost hear him crying over here," wrote one of Vermigli's friends after returning to England.

A map of Zurich around 1616. The location of Martyr's house is marked in red.

Zurich's Grossmünster church on the River Limmat, as it looks today. Built in the Middle Ages, it became a Protestant church in 1520. Martyr's house was behind it.

47

In spite of his old age, Martyr still wished he could have a child of his own. His friends suggested that he remarry. They recommended an Italian lady who had left her country to worship God freely. Her name was Caterina Merenda.

At sixty years of age, Martyr must have wondered if he had the energy to start a family, but he finally agreed. Martyr and Caterina married on May 9, 1559. In the first few years after their marriage, they had two children: first a son, then a daughter. They called the boy Eliperius and the girl Gerodora. Sadly, both children died days after birth, and Martyr was able to enjoy them for only a very short time.

From Zurich, he continued to write letters to encourage his friends in Italy and in England where, to his great joy, a Protestant queen—Elizabeth I—had come to the throne. His reputation as a competent and conscientious teacher kept growing, so he received official offers to teach both in England and at the University of Heidelberg. Also, the Reformer John Calvin invited him twice to pastor the Italian congregation at Geneva. Martyr, however, submitted to the authorities in his church who wanted him to keep his position.

Martyr was able to enjoy his children for only a very short time.

THE LAST YEARS

49

In September 1561, he was invited to an important meeting, called a colloquy, in the French city of Poissy, eighteen miles east of Paris. The meeting, sponsored by and presided over by the French ruler Catherine de' Medici, included both Protestant and Roman Catholic leaders who hoped to resolve the sharp and often violent conflict between the two groups. The leaders didn't come to an agreement even after a month of discussions, but Martyr's presence encouraged and strengthened the French Protestant church.

Martyr was also able to talk privately with Queen Catherine in their common mother tongue, Italian. They talked about many things—from the importance of being a godly ruler to the danger of attending Mass. When Catherine asked his advice on how to calm the troubled situation in her country, he told her to allow the Protestant churches to preach the gospel. If she did this, the truth would manifest itself.

Catherine de' Medici, engraving by Thomas Le Leu
NATIONAL GALLERY OF ART, GIFT OF JOHN O'BRIEN

Martyr was able to talk privately with Queen Catherine de' Medici in their common mother tongue, Italian.

THE LAST YEARS

Martyr returned to his teaching post in Zurich. By this time, he felt the weight of his age, but faithfully continued his work. One of his closest friends and students, Jerome Zanchi (pronounced ZAHN-key), called him "toothless but not speechless." Martyr tried to continue his college lessons even during a sudden illness, but finally had to give up. Soon, it was obvious he would not recover. Caterina was five months pregnant.

On his deathbed, he named a friend to watch over the baby and make sure he or she would not lack anything. He died on November 12, 1562. The next year, in May, Caterina gave birth to a baby girl. She was named Maria Vermiglia, maybe after Martyr's mother.

Martyr was sorely missed as a teacher and a writer, but what he had written continued to shape the Protestant Reformation in Europe and is still read, appreciated, and translated into many languages today.

Jerome Zanchi was Martyr's student in Lucca. In 1556, he reunited with Martyr in Strasbourg, where he taught at the same school.
WWW.MICHAELFINNEY.CO.UK

Martyr's influence as a teacher of the Scriptures also continued after his death. In Europe, a continent troubled by war and division, many of his students became good pastors or teachers, helping the Reformed church to find unity in Christ.

The Synod of Dort, an important meeting where Reformers clarified many of their teachings for the church in their day and for generations to come.
Vermigli's and Zanchi's writings played an important part in this meeting.

THE LAST YEARS

Time Line of Peter Martyr Vermigli's Life

1499, September 8–Martyr is born in Florence, Italy.

1511–Martyr's mother dies. He offers his services in the local church.

1514–He enters a monastery in Fiesole.

1518–He begins his studies at the University of Padua.

1526–He graduates, is appointed preacher, and preaches in different towns.

1530–He oversees a monastery in Bologna for three years, where he studies Hebrew with a Jewish physician.

1533–He becomes prior of a monastery in Spoleto.

1537–He moves to Naples, where he becomes familiar with Protestant teachings.

1540–He is suspended from preaching but is reinstated after an appeal.

1541–He is prior of the monastery of San Frediano in Lucca.

1542–He flees to Zurich, Switzerland. Since there is no work in Zurich, he moves to Basel. Later, Martin Bucer grants him a place as professor of Hebrew and Old Testament in Strasbourg, which was then in the Holy Roman Empire.

1545–He marries a French lady, Catherine Dammartin, a former nun.

1546–Beginning of the Schmalkaldic War.

1547–The English government, under King Edward VI, invites Martyr to teach at Oxford. He moves there ahead of his wife, Catherine, who joins him later.

1553–Catherine and King Edward VI die the same year. Mary Tudor comes to the throne after the brief reign of Lady Jane Grey.

1555–Martyr leaves England and returns to Strasbourg.

1556–He moves to Zurich.

1559–He marries the Italian Caterina Merenda. In the next two years, they have two children, who die soon after birth.

1561–He is invited to the Colloquy of Poissy to try to find common ground between Protestants and Roman Catholics. The attempts fail.

1562–He dies in Zurich, leaving his wife with child.

1563–His daughter Maria Vermiglia is born.

Did You Know?

- The first universities were usually founded and ruled by the students, who hired teachers and elected a rector (head of the university). The oldest university is the University of Bologna in Italy, founded in 1088. The University of Padua, where Vermigli studied, was founded in 1222. Many famous people studied there, including the astronomers Copernicus and Galileo.

- The school Martyr founded in Lucca included three levels of study. The first level was for children, who were taught Latin, Greek, and Hebrew so they could one day study the Scriptures. In the second level, Martyr taught young people to understand the letters of the apostle Paul by reading them in the original Greek text. After each class, he would ask one of the students to summarize the lesson. The third level of teaching consisted of evening classes on the Psalms for adults.

- Traveling in the sixteenth century could be quite dangerous, especially in unfamiliar areas where people spoke an unknown language. Normally people traveled by foot, on horseback, or by boat. Travelers on foot normally carried a stick and a map. If they had to move merchandise or furniture, they used horse-drawn carts or had their belongings shipped through professional carriers. It was very common for bags to be lost, damaged, or stolen.

  A person walking by foot on a plain road without obstacles could usually travel about twelve miles per day. Hitchhiking was common. That distance could be at least doubled by riding a horse. Boats were even faster. A person traveling by river could cover more than sixty miles per day.

There were many inns along the way, but they were not always clean. German and English inns had a reputation for being the cleanest, while Italian and French inns had a reputation for serving good food. Inns could also be noisy because many people visited them at night to drink and have fun. Thieves liked to stay around inns. If they noticed that a traveler had money, they would try to rob him during the night.

Traveling over the Alps was particularly difficult. Sometimes, travelers had to attach some iron crampons to their shoes in order to cross icy areas. For travelers on foot, the descent was the most dangerous portion of the trip (it is easier to slip going down). Horses, however, tended to slip more easily on the way up.

❦ Martyr never learned to speak German or English very well. All university students spoke Latin, so he wrote and taught in that language. That way, he could be understood by any learned person anywhere in Europe.

❦ Catherine Vermigli had an unusual hobby: she liked to carve plum stones into funny and interesting faces.

❦ Martyr's teachings on the Lord's Supper had a great influence on other Christians of his time. John Calvin said, "The whole doctrine of the Eucharist [Lord's Supper] was crowned by Peter Martyr, who left nothing more to be done." This doctrine was later summarized in the Heidelberg Catechism:

Question 76. What does it mean to eat the crucified body and drink the shed blood of Christ?

Answer. It means not only to embrace with a believing heart all the sufferings and death of Christ, and thereby to obtain the forgiveness of sins and life eternal, but moreover, also, to be so united more and more to His sacred body by the Holy Spirit, who dwells both in Christ and in us, that, although He is in heaven and we on earth, we are nevertheless flesh of His flesh and bone of His bone, and live and are governed forever by one Spirit, as members of the same body are governed by one soul.

- Children in the sixteenth century liked to play as much as you do. As they grew, however, they were encouraged to spend less time playing and more time working or studying, depending on how much money the family had. Poor children made toys out of common things like sticks or reeds, strings, fruit pits, or nuts. Those who lived in well-to-do families learned to play chess and checkers, which were considered useful for training the mind.

  Boys had homemade toy soldiers and toy swords, hobbyhorses, stilts, bowling pins, and wheels (to push with a stick) and liked to play catch or leapfrog. Girls had dolls or played simple musical instruments like flutes or tambourines. Flutes were often made out of reeds or animal bones. All children liked tops, balls, marbles, pinwheels, and games like blindman's bluff or hide-and-seek.

- The Reformers paid much attention to the education of their children, teaching them to read and memorize the Scriptures as early as possible. For example, Rebecca Hooper, daughter of the English Reformer John Hooper, learned to read when she was four. Around that time, she memorized the Lord's Prayer, the Apostles' Creed, the Ten Commandments, the first two psalms, and a prayer of thanksgiving in only three months. After that, she started to memorize the catechism.

- Catherine de' Medici launched many new fashions in France. For example, she wore high heels at her wedding because she was very short. The fashion caught on, and Queen Mary I of England adopted them as well. Catherine is also thought to be the first to use a folding fan in France.

❦ The toilet, as we know it, was invented in 1596 by the godson of Queen Elizabeth I of England. Before that, it was just a hole in the ground, either in a portion of the house or in a small room outside. Soap was created in England in the fourteenth century. Even though it was commonly used in the sixteenth century, Anna Bullinger, in a letter to her son, had to remind him that his shirts "must be soaped."

❦ Bullinger courted his wife, Anna, while she was still a nun in a convent. In those days, usually when men wanted to court a woman, they would make arrangements to meet her through a relative or friend. Bullinger managed his courtship himself, persuading Anna that being a wife and a mother was the best calling she could have. Later, he wrote a love song for their wedding. Since neither of them wanted a big celebration, they married quietly and in private at their dinner table with a pastor to preside over their wedding.

What Happened to the Others?

Gian Pietro Carafa (Pope Paul IV) died in 1559. His violence against Protestants and Jews was so fierce that, when he died, people decapitated his statue and dragged the head through the streets until they threw it in the Tiber River. He has been called the most hated pope in history.

Before marrying Martin Bucer, **Wibrandis** was married to three other men—all Protestants—who each died of illness after a few years of marriage. Their names were Ludwig Keller, Johann Oecolampadius, and Wolfgang Capito. From these marriages, she had nine children. In 1541 a deadly illness struck the area where they lived, and Wolfgang and three children died. The same illness killed Martin Bucer's wife Elizabeth. Before dying, Elizabeth asked her husband to marry Wibrandis so that the two of them could take care of each other. Martin and Wibrandis married in 1542 and had two children. When Martin died in 1551, Wibrandis, then forty-seven years old, took the family back to her hometown of Basel, where she continued to care for her children until she died in 1563 from an illness.

Julius Terentianus's wife, **Anna**, died in 1562, seven months before Martyr. After Martyr's death, Julius worked for a while as a proofreader in a printer's workshop that published Protestant books. We don't know when Julius died.

When Martyrillus (**Martyr Terentianus**) grew up, he became an ordained pastor, got married, and was vice principal of a school in Winthertur, Switzerland. He died in 1585.

Catherine de' Medici never managed to bring peace between Roman Catholics and Protestants. In fact, things became much worse. In 1572, after the marriage of the king's sister Margaret to Protestant Henry III of Navarre (who later became Henry IV of France), thousands of Protestants were killed in Paris. This bloodshed, known as the St. Bartholomew's Day Massacre, lasted for over a week and claimed the lives of many French Protestant leaders. Catherine has often been blamed for this massacre, but nothing is sure. She died in 1589 when she was almost eighty years old.

Jerome Zanchi was asked to take Martyr's place in Zurich, but he didn't think he could match his teacher. After pastoring an Italian Protestant church in Switzerland, he was invited to teach at the University of Heidelberg, where he stayed for nine years. His writings and teachings became influential.

Maria Vermiglia stayed in Zurich, got married, and had thirteen children.

The bodies of **Martin Bucer** and **Catherine Vermigli** lay peacefully in their graves until Queen Mary I decided to bring to a court trial every Protestant who lived or had lived in England. If they were found guilty of teaching something contrary to Roman Catholic doctrines, their bodies (living or dead) would be burned as a symbol of the fires of hell.

Bucer's body was dug up, chained to a pole, and burned. Catherine's body was also dug up, but the court couldn't find any proof against her. Her body was then thrown on a dung heap, where it remained for five years. When Elizabeth I became queen, Catherine's bones were buried again. Before closing the tomb, however, her bones were mixed with those of an English princess named Frideswide, who had been made a saint by the Roman Catholic Church. Since St. Frideswide's bones were considered so holy that they possessed miraculous powers, no Roman Catholic would have tampered with them.

> In the course of a long interrogation and trial, the government officials forced **Thomas Cranmer** to deny his faith and to sign several documents showing his full support of the Roman Catholic Church. In spite of this, they condemned him to death for his central role in leading the Protestant Reformation in England and asked him to write a public speech he would recite publicly before his execution in Oxford.
>
> By the time he read the speech, however, Cranmer had repented of what he had done. He started to follow what he had written, but then shocked the authorities by rejecting not his Protestant writings, but the documents he had been forced to sign. Before he could be stopped, he denounced the pope as "Christ's enemy, and Antichrist with all his false doctrine."
>
> Furious, the authorities took him through the streets of Oxford to the place where other Reformers had been executed a few months earlier. They mounted him on a pile of wood and lit the fire. In a final demonstration of repentance, Cranmer stretched out over the fire the hand he had used to sign his declaration of loyalty to the Roman Catholic Church. "Forasmuch as my hand offended, writing contrary to my heart, my hand shall first be punished," he said. His last words were taken from Stephen's final speech in Acts 7:56, 59, "I see the heavens opened, and the Son of man standing on the right hand of God.... Lord Jesus, receive my spirit."

From Peter Martyr's Pen

The Peace of God

The peace of the world removes external troubles but does not change people. They remain in their desperation, darkness, bad conscience, and sins. The peace of God is then more effective, because it protects us from a present and dangerous adversary, and changes us. It makes the fearful bold, the timid brave and the weak strong. When through faith we lay hold of Christ, nothing can stand in the way of us who are joined to him. Instead, we say, "The Lord is my strength; I will not fear what man may do to me. If an armed camp rises up against me, I will not lose hope."

—from sermon on John 20:19–23

The Word of God

As you know, gold and jewels shine brighter the more our hands rub them. You are not unaware that the Word of God surpasses gold, topaz and all precious stones in brightness. We are taught that the words of God are similar to those living waters which not only fully quench our thirst but spring up to eternal life and that well water becomes more pure and tasty the more it is stirred and hauled up. Since the divine statements are like a consuming fire which, the more it is stirred up and blown upon, the more it flares up with larger and brighter flames. Hence we too will possess deeper pleasure and delight the more fully we celebrate the excellence of the divine wisdom by our oration

—from inaugural oration at Zurich

From Peter Martyr Vermigli, *Life, Letters, and Sermons*, trans. and ed. John Patrick Donnelly, S.J., Sixteenth Century Essays and Studies (Kirksville, Mo.: Truman State University), 230, 213. The quotations on page 44 have also been paraphrased or taken from this translation.

Acknowledgments

I have many people to thank—starting with my pastor, Rev. Michael Brown, who has encouraged me to write about Peter Martyr Vermigli. I am grateful to my publisher, Dr. Joel Beeke, and all the staff at Reformation Heritage Books for their encouragement, guidance, and patience.

I am deeply grateful for my illustrator, Joel Spector, who graciously persevered in his commitment to produce high quality illustrations in spite of a sudden and terminal illness that took his life soon after the task was completed, and to his wife, Rowena, who supported him in this endeavor. These illustrations will always have a special meaning to me.

I also want to thank Dr. Emidio Campi, emeritus professor at the University of Zurich and one of the leading scholars on Vermigli; author and researcher Giulio Orazio Bravi, who is also founder of the Protestant Cultural Center in Bergamo, Italy; and Daniel Borvan, doctoral student in Reformation history at Oxford University, for reading my manuscript and answering many of my questions.

Once again, I received much help from my Sunday school students, Lucy Plotner, Evan Olow, Israel Brindis De Salas, Iain Brown, Isaac and Caleb Stone, and Isaiah Hasten, who listened to a reading of the manuscript and asked the most unexpected and interesting questions.

Finally, a big thanks to my husband, Tom, and my kids, who regularly and patiently listen to my frequent and endless stories about Reformers, kings, popes, and queens.